Student-Oriented Curriculum:
A Remarkable Journey of Discovery

Student-Oriented Curriculum
A Remarkable Journey of Discovery

Wallace M. Alexander
with Dennis Carr & Kathy McAvoy

National Middle School Association
Westerville, Ohio

National Middle School Association
4151 Executive Parkway, Suite 300
Westerville, OH 43081
1-800-528-NMSA

Copyright ©2006, 1995 by National Middle School Association

The materials presented in this publication are the expressions of the authors and do not necessarily represent the policies of NMSA.

NMSA is a registered servicemark of National Middle School Association. Printed in the United States of America.

Sue Swaim, Executive Director
Jeff Ward, Deputy Executive Director
April Tibbles, Director of Publications
Edward Brazee, Editor, Professional Publications
John Lounsbury, Consulting Editor, Professional Publications
Mary Mitchell, Designer, Editorial Assistant
Mark Shumaker, Graphic Designer
Dawn Williams, Publications Manager
Marcia Meade-Hurst, Senior Publications Representative

Library of Congress Cataloging-in-Publication Data
Alexander, Wallace M.
.   Student-oriented curriculum: a remarkable journey of discovery/
by Wallace M. Alexander with Dennis Carr, Kathy McAvoy.
        p. cm.
    Includes bibliographical references.
    ISBN-13: 978-1-56090-197-6 (pbk.)
    ISBN-10: 1-56090-197-7 (pbk.)
        1. Middle school education--United States. 2. Student participation in curriculum planning--United States. 3. Student-centered learning--United States. I. Carr, Dennis. II. McAvoy, Kathy. III. Title.

LB1623.5.A428 2006
373.236--dc22   2006046650

*To these young adolescents
who taught us so much…*

CONTENTS

FOREWORD

What happens when a good middle school team has the typical middle school components—a flexible block schedule, heterogeneous grouping, advisory program, and various exploratory activities—and yet is still dissatisfied with students' learning? Easy, they move to student-oriented curriculum as the next logical step. But only the answer is easy; for the doing of "student-oriented" curriculum is the hard part, made more difficult by the uncertainty of just what student-oriented curriculum means and entails.

This book combines the stances of several other excellent publications on curriculum integration in middle level schools. Most fall into one of two categories—those that tell how to create integrative curriculum and those that describe examples of various integrated curriculum activities. *Student-Oriented Curriculum: A Remarkable Journey of Discovery* does both as it explains the process one team used to make learning more relevant and meaningful for young adolescents. While we thereby learn a great deal about what they did, we learn even more about how and why they did it.

Alexander allows us insight into the deliberations, discussions, and often painful negotiations that took place around each of the changes these teachers made. This inside look into teachers' thinking as they leave the safe and comfortable teacher-directed, predetermined curriculum to involve and challenge students is the value of this book. For it is in these conversations that we understand the real struggles and the real triumphs of their work.

Kathy McAvoy and Dennis Carr intended to make what originally was a daily, integrated studies block into "the curriculum." This is no "let's-try-it-because-it-is-the-end-of-the-year-unit." These teachers aren't doing an obligatory interdisciplinary unit because it is the current thing to do. As the author explains, "The goal was for this block to become completely integrative, with students brainstorming themes, activities, and resources. The ultimate goal was to have this become the whole curriculum." By the year's end they had largely succeeded.

The beauty of this book is that it, like *Watershed: A Successful Voyage Into Integrative Learning* (Springer, 1994) and *Soundings: A Democratic, Student-Centered Education* (Springer, 2006) is a prime example of a fully integrative program. While many teachers tinker with the curriculum by taking tiny steps away from separate subjects, this partnership made a commitment to improving learning for young adolescents by leaving the status quo rather dramatically.

Student-Oriented Curriculum reads like a story—engaging, witty, and insightful. Solid in the understanding about the type of learning that young adolescents should experience and written in an extremely readable style, it gives readers practical advice on all facets of integrated curriculum. In the context of the units described, the reader is able to follow the team's planning as they both work to solve scheduling problems, work with reluctant parents and colleagues, decide how their new and evolving curriculum fits with the required one, and allow students to find their comfort zones with ever-increasing responsibilities. The reflections of students, located throughout the text, add an additional touch of reality and validity.

While still obligated to use the traditional grade card, the teachers had to consider how to measure student learning when students were doing different things at different times. They planned assessment strategies that were parts of the ongoing teaching and learning process and actively involved the students. Assessment activities were viewed as opportunities for students to discover their strengths and weaknesses.

An essential aspect of this focus was on student self-assessment, which came about when teachers learned to ask the right questions and help students develop legitimate assessment criteria. Key components of student self-assessment described are weekly self-evaluations, reflective journals, daily plans written by students, weekly conferences, product and presentation assessments, grade conferences, and family conferences directed by students. Each of these tools is described with examples of assessment rubrics given.

This book answers the recurring questions about seriousness of purpose, academic integrity, and rigor that any discussion of integrative curriculum inevitably engenders. No one reading this book can miss these themes that run through every chapter as both students and teachers reflect on the powerful learning that occurred. At one point, describing several group inquiry projects initiating a school-wide recycling project, investigating the relationship between various methods of forest harvesting and wildlife habitat, and exploring endangered species, Alexander muses, "And some say these kids aren't concerned about important issues!" More than anything else, we see in this book just how serious and intellectually challenging this type of work is for students and their teachers.

As helpful as the descriptions of the various units are and the planning process that brought them to fruition, perhaps the most useful and powerful part of this book is the identification and description of 16 lessons learned. In this section the simple-complex nature of integrative curriculum becomes apparent as we recognize that these conclusions are neither a scope and sequence nor a cookbook for change. Rather, the lessons represent what we know to be true when changes are made, ones that begin with changing our beliefs, even before we change any of our practices. This section is a primer for those serious about integrative curricula. Readers may want to read this especially significant chapter first. Here you will find the framework around which the rest of the book revolves.

Alexander and the teacher team he writes about are excellent examples of the practitioner-scholars who challenge young adolescents in real settings. *Student-Oriented Curriculum* is as useful today as when it was first published 11 years ago, a valuable contribution to the body of literature that explores the difficult, challenging, yet rewarding task of matching young adolescent needs to curriculum. We are grateful to Wally Alexander for writing *Student-Oriented Curriculum* originally and to Kathy McAvoy and Dennis Carr for their leadership with curriculum integration over the years. It is interesting to read the recent reflections of these educators more than a decade after they began their "remarkable journey" and to hear that the lessons learned are still valid for young adolescents and middle level schools today.

—Edward N. Brazee

JULY						
				1	2	3
4	5	6	7	8	9	10
11	12	13	14	15	16	17
18	19	20	21	22	23	24
25	26	27	28	29	30	31

An idea whose time came

Two courageous teachers successfully carried out a year-long experiment in student-oriented curriculum. Here is their story that began as a project for a graduate class at the University of Maine. After a year of intensive study of middle school philosophy and practices, I was "chomping at the bit" to try out my ideas with some real kids in a real school. My original proposal was to work with Kathy McAvoy and Dennis Carr, a pair of dedicated, progressive middle level educators, who made up the sixth-grade team at Mt. Jefferson Junior High, a small, rural middle school in Lee, Maine. This team was to implement an integrated studies approach in a designated daily block, with the long-range goal of having that block grow to become "the curriculum."

In preparation, Kathy, Dennis, and I spent several weeks working together during the summer, a week at the Middle Level Education Institute at the University of Maine and two more weeks at a Foxfire Level I class. My role with this team was to provide support, generate ideas for thematic topics, make connections with potential guest speakers, offer reassurance that they were doing the right thing, and give the slight push that would convince Kathy and Dennis that now was the time to "take the plunge." I was involved in planning, implementing, and assessing this new curriculum. As it turned out, for me, this project became the focus of a year's research into student-centered learning, integrative curriculum, authentic assessment, and student empowerment.

For several years, Kathy and Dennis had discussed the necessity of the middle level curriculum's becoming more responsive to the needs of young adolescents. These veteran teachers had acknowledged the importance of linking the subject areas and relating the curriculum to the interests of the students and the world around them. When principal Martha Witham, a dynamic, instructional leader, saw the possibility for this sixth-grade team's leading the rest of the school toward developing a curriculum that would be relevant to the students and responsive to their various non-academic needs, she was most supportive.

The project would provide an opportunity for students to study thematic units, working cooperatively to integrate all subject areas within a daily block of time. Since this was a novel idea for the students as well as the teachers, several days at the beginning of the school year were devoted to working on social skills, trust building, team building, decision making, and modeling the student-generated curriculum process. Plans for the initial unit on the environment included choices of activities as examples of the range of activities that can be part of this type of curriculum. We were not sure how strictly to adhere to these unit plans but wanted to have them in hand if needed. The block eventually would become the whole curriculum, completely integrative, with students brainstorming themes, activities, and resources.

In the interest of fairness to readers of this book who are challenged in schools with organizational structures that make curriculum change very difficult, I must point out that the team described here already had several very significant organizational pieces in place before attempting this change. It had experience with a completely flexible block schedule, heterogeneous grouping, advisory programs, and portfolio assessment. More importantly, Kathy and Dennis had worked as a two-teacher or partner team for several years. For them, the move to student-oriented curriculum was simply a matter of taking the next logical step.

Here you will follow the story of two dynamic teachers and a group of young adolescents who took risks to find a better way of learning. It tells of their challenges, successes, failures, frustrations, and revelations. Thoughtful reflections by students and the teaching team will allow readers to learn even more about the process and outcomes of student-oriented curriculum. ♦

PREPARING FOR IMPLEMENTATION

AUGUST						
1	2	3	4	5	6	7
8	9	10	11	12	13	14
15	16	17	18	19	20	21
22	23	24	25	26	27	28
29	30	31				

How do we start this thing?

While this project started as an experiment in integrative curriculum, inevitably it grew into one of empowering students in every aspect of their learning and classroom life. Like a rocket taking off, the energy expended to get started was immense; but the more we progressed, the more students became invested and involved in their own learning. Eventually our autopilot took over as we learned to trust each other; then we sat back, loosened our seatbelts a bit, and enjoyed the ride.

One of the most difficult parts was deciding where to start. Much of our early planning discussion revolved around how much of the school day would be devoted to this project, how much power would be shared with students, and what kinds of skills the students would initially need. While everyone agreed on the goal of a completely integrative curriculum that solicited student voice, the teachers were not ready to walk in the first day of school without some definite plans. They felt that the students would need some preparation for making decisions and working cooperatively. As it turned out, they were right—it took several weeks to break the students' mind-set that teachers make the important decisions and then tell students what they need to know to pass the tests.

A major step was to decide how far Kathy and Dennis could go without forcing them too far out of their comfort zones. It was decided that initially, one of the three 100-minute blocks each day would be devoted to integrated studies while maintaining a more traditional curriculum—a literacy block, including reading, writing, and word processing, and a math and social studies block—during the rest of the day. It was also decided that the first theme would be the environment, which permitted the teachers to plan some activities and locate resources. While the intent was to build in as much student choice and involvement as possible, it was critical to model a variety of activities for students to counteract their past experiences of primarily teacher-directed curriculum and instruction. Additional time was spent on ways to initiate the students to a dramatically different school experience and discussing an endless array of "what-ifs."

Although I am listed as author, I want to make it explicitly clear whose story this book tells. While I had a deep interest and involvement in this project, and these are my words describing it, this story does not belong to me. This story belongs to Kathy McAvoy, Dennis Carr, and 40 exciting, creative young people who spent a school year as sixth graders at Mount Jefferson Junior High School. The accomplishments of these people, teachers and students, far exceeded my expectations. The middle school theories do work, and the results were astounding! My hope is that you, the reader, can absorb a portion of what these people have taught me about teaching, learning, and themselves. My hope is that this story will help you face the risks and challenges of change and encourage you to "take the plunge." ♦

TEAM BUILDING

SEPTEMBER						
			1	2	3	4
5	6	7	8	9	10	11
12	13	14	15	16	17	18
19	20	21	22	23	24	25
26	27	28	29	30		

Overcoming the gravitational pull of years of passivity

During the first two weeks of the school year, the integrated block was devoted to team and trust building, developing social skills and decision-making skills, along with modeling of the brainstorming process. We intermixed brainstorming sessions with activities that allowed for physical movement (drawing on ideas found in Project Adventure, 1986). With students coming from three elementary schools, we concentrated on helping everyone become well acquainted and comfortable with one another. We also worked on the social skills needed to work effectively in groups and the dynamics of having 40 sixth graders brainstorming in one room (early attempts were admittedly rather chaotic). Two successful activities follow.

Portraits

Pairs interview each other and produce a portrait of their partners using words or drawings. Finished portraits are presented to the whole group as each student is introduced by his or her partner. Portraits can then be displayed and new things added as they are discovered. Students

7

were asked to choose partners they didn't know very well, someone from a different elementary school.

Shining moments

We started this activity in advisory groups (12-14 students). In groups of three, we discussed memorable experiences in school—things that happened during our school lives that were especially effective, had lasting affect, or influenced our future. Individuals shared their shining moments. We then brainstormed a list of the characteristics that made these lessons special. The lists from the trials were compared and compiled. Things that appeared on more than one list were identified: *... the lesson was fun, ... it was outside the school building, ... it was hands-on, ... the work was something other than regular schoolwork, ... the activity was my idea, ... we had a choice, ... it was interesting to me, ... it was important and "real."*

These characteristics of effective lessons became guidelines as we collaborated on curriculum throughout the year. The most interesting thing about this activity for me is that no matter how many times it is conducted, with adults or with kids, the list of characteristics of memorable lessons is always essentially the same. We all know what works—why aren't we doing it?

Brainstorming sessions soon moved into discussions of the first theme, "The Environment." We started with these two questions: What do you know about the environment? and What would you like to know about the environment?

Since whole-group brainstorming was still rough at this point, lists were generated in two groups of 20 and then followed up in the total group for comparison and consolidation.

From the lists of what the students wanted to know, we engaged in a free-flowing exchange of ideas for activities that might help us obtain the desired knowledge. We also discussed the fact that the teachers, of necessity, had some "givens" for this unit. From a combination of student brainstorming and teachers' givens, the following action plan for our study of the environment emerged.

FIGURE I
Environment Unit Activities

1) Everyone will do an environmental vocabulary log:
   Write and illustrate these terms

ozone layer	recycling	acid rain
water cycle	habitat	erosion
niche	adaptation	ecology
extinction	life cycle	ecosystem
continental drift	fauna	food chain
flora	fossil	species
pollution	topsoil	community
endangered species	mammal	clear cutting (forests)
natural selection	pesticide	herbicide
photosynthesis		

2) Everyone will keep a daily journal (plans, goals, and reflections) and a working portfolio.
3) Everyone will complete a writing piece: predicting the future of our environment (with scientific basis).
4) Everyone will participate in a mapping activity.
5) Everyone will research an endangered species and prepare a one page report. All reports will be combined and published in the form of a book.
6) Everyone will complete an individual or group "inquiry" on an environmental topic of his or her choice. Final products may vary. Each inquiry will include at least one business letter (per person) requesting information, at least one live interview (per person) requesting information, and references from literature on the topic.
7) Possible community service project. (Clean-up in each community?)
8) Possible mini-conference day with guest speakers.

This action plan, as well as all subsequent ones, included both individual assignments to be completed by all students and an inquiry element in which small groups could pursue in-depth answers to questions of personal interest within the theme.

During these first two weeks of school, students were also introduced to the concept of a weekly reflection/self-evaluation report (see Assessment, p. 19).

The time spent on team building, trust, and cooperation during these first two weeks was critical. It paid major dividends throughout the remainder of the year. To assume that these behaviors would have evolved without a concentrated effort would be a mistake. ◆

THE
ENVIRONMENT UNIT

SEPTEMBER						
			1	2	3	4
5	6	7	8	9	10	11
12	13	14	15	16	17	18
19	20	21	22	23	24	25
26	27	28	29	30		

Entering the stratosphere

Forming groups for inquiry projects was left to student choice. In most cases this was successful the first time. Two groups didn't work out, eventually dissolved, and were rearranged—another learning experience for all involved. This led to interesting discussions about making a commitment to the group and the process of finding people who had common interests with whom to work. To begin formulating plans for inquiries, groups answered the following questions:

1) Who is in our group?
2) What is the major topic for our inquiry?
3) What do we want to know about our topic?
4) Where will we get our information?
5) Who will do what?
6) What activities will we do?
7) What could we do for a final product or project?
8) How will we teach the others about this topic?

Teachers tried to facilitate this activity without expressing too many of their own opinions. At this point in the year the teachers' opinions were still perceived by students as the accepted ones. We wanted the students to come up with their own ideas. Each group answered these questions and submitted them for our inspection. Some were very good, while others needed a little help. The result provided a rough draft of a plan. Groups were then asked to prepare a formal proposal for their inquiry.

One of the first things the students discovered was that they were expected to schedule their own time during the integrated studies block. While teachers provided weekly and long-term objectives and deadlines, it was up to the students to decide when they would work on individual and group projects. They had to work around the absence of some people because of intramurals, chorus, band, and other activities. Most responded well to this challenge, while a few needed guidance, providing a wonderful lesson in time management. Students eventually became very good at balancing and using class and small group time.

Whole-group brainstorming sessions continued on an as-needed basis, usually at least once a week, and became a forum to air student and teacher concerns. At one of these sessions about two weeks into the first unit, the concept of classroom norms or rules was introduced. We intentionally waited to introduce this topic until the students had started working in groups and had a chance to see some of the difficulties that developed. After a few days, they had identified some problems and could see the need for rules, in fact they were asking for them. As became the practice throughout the year, this issue was brought directly to the students. They discussed classroom norms in small groups, then brought suggestions to the whole-group session. Individual norms were identified and voted upon, and an official list of norms was compiled. Nothing was added unless all agreed they could live with it. The list of adopted classroom norms follows:

1) Students (and teachers) can raise hands if room gets too noisy.
2) Use 20-inch voice.

3) Keep your hands to yourself.
4) Don't bother others when they are working.
5) Respect other people and their property.
6) Nothing in your mouth.
7) Take turns talking and listen while others speak.

At a follow-up session, these sixth graders decided on appropriate consequences for people who disregarded the classroom norms. Once again, decisions had to be unanimous. They also decided they should be able to monitor their norms and set up a system of student monitors. Results were immediate and dramatic. They were very hard on themselves and each other. The whole issue of monitoring went through a lengthy evolution resulting in greatly increased individual awareness of what is acceptable behavior. We would never have reached the level of behavior eventually enjoyed if we had mandated these same rules.

Another early lesson dealt with resources. The students couldn't believe we weren't going to tell them everything they needed to know. We were pleased to help guide them, but the main responsibility for locating resources became their job. They were encouraged to write letters, make phone calls, conduct interviews, and look to community members as sources of information. They also conducted traditional library research, consulted CD ROM encyclopedias, and eventually linked with other schools through the Internet. While we were initially worried about locating community resources in our very rural area, we discovered there is a wealth of information out there. We also found the local people very responsive when students asked for their assistance.

About three weeks into the unit on the environment, we had two breakthroughs in one day—our first guest speaker and a small group field trip. Both of these activities were completely student generated. Brian, whose group inquiry dealt with forest management and harvesting, had written to a local contractor for information. This gentleman graciously volunteered to speak to the whole sixth grade. Brian phoned the speaker, made all the arrangements, and acted as host for the speaker while he was at the school. The session was a huge success. Everyone was impressed with the quality of the questions raised and the relationships students discovered between forest management and other environmental issues.

That same day, a group of five students toured local forest harvesting operations with another local forester who was also a member of the school board and a sixth-grade parent. The students were presented with great lessons on various forest harvesting methods and how wildlife is affected by these different practices. Once again, all information was shared with the whole group upon return to the school. During the sharing sessions, all students were attentive, interested, and prepared with relevant questions for the returning field-trippers.

These two activities generated an explosion of interest in speakers and trips—exactly what we had been waiting for. It would have been easy for us to arrange resource speakers and trips, but we wanted the kids to discover these things on their own. **The power of ownership cannot be overstated.** After that day, guests and field trips became common. All contacts and arrangements, including transportation, were made by the students and all new information shared with the whole group. These young people were starting to learn about much more than the content related to the environment. The communication skills, letter writing, phone calls, interviewing, surveying, hosting of guests, planning and executing trips, designing questions to ask, and sharing information with the rest of the class all became the students' responsibility; and the related skills were learned within the context of students' pursuit of answers to their own questions.

Instruction by the teachers during this unit usually took the form of mini-lessons with small groups at the time they needed skills or information. There was also a great deal of peer teaching going on. It was common to see students sharing information about resources, newly learned computer skills, and various other items of information with others. Instruction, while somewhat informal, became truly cooperative. Since the teachers were, to a large extent, freed from presenting information to the whole class, they were able to meet and confer with smaller groups, monitor progress, and give individual instruction as needed. **One-on-one contact with students increased greatly.** Issues that needed to be addressed with groups or individuals often emerged from the weekly self-evaluations.

Some of the highlights of this first unit follow. An all day, school-wide, environmental summit organized and hosted by the sixth grade grew from an interest in bringing in community speakers. It turned out to be a wonderful day for all involved. The student body was put into multi-aged groups and circulated through six 40-minute presentations by a local recycling group, a forester, a state biologist who spoke on endangered species in Maine, a paper company forester, a groundwater expert, and a group of high school science students. Individual teachers gave their students different assignments. Every student assessment at the end of the day was very favorable. I expected to see many students comment on the day's being an enjoyable change of pace, but I was a little surprised at how many remarked about the learning that had taken place. Over half the evaluations included comments about the things they learned, and many mentioned how effective learning can take place without sitting still in rows, doing worksheets, and reading textbooks. This was obviously a very productive day for the kids, but I think the other teachers in the school may have received a message also. This summit proved to be an effective way to model to some very traditional teachers how different kinds of activities can result in real learning.

Of particular interest was the group of high school students who presented some engaging environmental simulations to the middle school students. It's incredible how the middle schoolers look up to these older adolescents and respond to what they have to say. What a resource to tap into! It was refreshing to see older students modeling an academic endeavor, spreading their enthusiasm, and transmitting the message that learning is fun and "cool." We found it interesting to see the response from our kids, but even more fascinating to see the reaction of the high schoolers. You could see their self-esteem growing throughout the day. We may have helped ignite an interest in teaching in these seniors. They obviously felt great about what they did and the way our kids responded. They got a taste of the best part of teaching young adolescents.

At the end of this unit, groups presented their inquiry projects to the rest of the class. Everyone had to participate in this presentation, but groups made all decisions as to who did what, and individuals could do what they were comfortable with. This turned out to be enjoyable and very educational for all involved. Everyone, teachers and students alike, shared responsibility for assessing these presentations. Students took this responsibility very seriously, and it helped keep everyone focused and involved. All presentations were videotaped for later viewing by students and parents.

Group inquiry projects included the initiation of a school-wide recycling program, investigation into the relationship between various forest harvesting methods and wildlife habitat, exploration of endangered species, a study of community recycling, and local water-quality testing.

Our culminating event for this unit was an Environmental Fair. Students' work was showcased, providing them an audience beyond their teachers and classmates. Students prepared displays and were ready to explain their work and answer questions. This early evening event was open to the public and very well attended; nearly every student arrived with his or her entire family. It was a learning experience for all. Students, teachers, and parents mingled and talked about the projects and the integrated studies block in general. The video of student presentations was a hit. This evening belonged to the kids; and they savored it, radiating pride. This event ended any lingering doubts any of us had about the validity of the student-oriented approach to curriculum.

While these sixth graders were openly skeptical and somewhat reluctant at the beginning of the change to a student-oriented curriculum, their remarks at the end of the first theme sampled below, speak to their enthusiasm at this initial stage of curriculum integration and involvement.

It was nice for a change to think about how we wanted to learn instead of how we had to learn. I think we would not have learned as much if we had done 50 worksheets and 15 tests.

———————————

I liked studying the environment. It was neat. I wouldn't change anything. Cool. I loved it. It was fun, especially when we went around to the different classrooms. My favorite was the one on forestry. It was awesome. I liked doing recycling.

———————————

I think we should have some young students from the University of Maine. And have them come in and see how much we have learned. I think they would be surprised to see how much knowledge that sixth graders can get by themselves and use it to get a project together that is really good.

———————————

I liked it because I learned a lot about animals and trees. I liked the self-assessment because it was neat to go back over what I did.

———————————

I like picking your own topic and not getting told that you have to do this. It was cool. I liked learning about recycling.

———————————

I liked the environmental unit because we could choose our topic like clear cutting. We also got to make field trips and stuff like we got to choose our project and our partners so it was fun. I liked that we had group time and individual time and we got to go outside and get stuff we needed.

I liked learning about all the animals that I did and I liked the projects other people did. It was fun. I liked evaluating myself because we never got to do that before and you get to argue with the teacher and not get in trouble for it.

I liked the environmental unit, it made you learn more about what's happening in the world. I also liked how we made our own decision who we were working with. I think people worked good, but I like how you have to work with a different person each time, because you see how good other people work and meet other people.

I wouldn't change anything cause I just look at all the things we learned and did. I can think of the fun things and I can think of a lot of them. I think that we should have integrated throughout the years to come. ◆

ASSESSMENT

OCTOBER						
					1	2
3	4	5	6	7	8	9
10	11	12	13	14	15	16
17	18	19	20	21	22	23
24	25	26	27	28	29	30

Inertia is taking over

As we started this curriculum experiment, one of our biggest concerns was assessment. How were we going to measure student learning with 40 students when they weren't doing the same thing at the same time? Beyond this problem, we wanted assessment to be authentic—but we were obligated to continue using a very traditional grade card.

Our assessment goals included the following.

1. There should be no distinction between teaching, learning, and assessment.

2. Assessment should be continuous and ongoing. It should be an integrated part of every school day, not something that happens only at the end of a unit.

3. Assessment should not exist to point out student weaknesses, but should be an opportunity for students to reflect on their learning and discover their strengths.

4. Assessment must be student centered. Students are the best judges of their own work. If they are going to become

responsible for their own learning, they must also be responsible for assessment.

This all sounds good, but how is it put into practice? Even after we decided to stress self-assessment, we weren't exactly sure how it should be done. We needed help.

One of our greatest resources proved to be our network of "Foxfire" teachers. "Foxfire" philosophy, derived from the works of John Dewey by Eliot Wigginton, emphasizes student empowerment and recognizes reflection as one of the most crucial and neglected aspects of public education. Conversations with "Foxfire" colleagues led us to understand that implementing self-assessment involves asking the right questions. This is analogous to Jim Beane's (1993) approach to selection of curriculum themes. Beane would never ask students, "What do you want to study?" Themes are selected through a series of "back-door" questions: "What things concern you personally?" "What are your concerns with the world around you?" "How does the world affect you?" Correspondingly, with self-assessment you can't just ask kids what they should get for a grade. **You must lead them, by asking the right questions, to development of legitimate assessment criteria**.

One of the most useful resources was ASCD's, *Expanding Student Assessment* (1991), especially the chapter by Rieneke Zessoules and Howard Gardner. These authors present a thoughtful look at assessment that has real implications for teachers interested in initiating student self-evaluation. They view assessment as an integral part of the learning process, not as an isolated piece we drop on students once in a while. They also see reflection as fundamental to authentic assessment, a vital element that is missing in most classrooms. We felt that they could have written this piece expressly to address our personal assessment concerns.

With this background, we made preliminary plans to implement self-assessment. Eventually we went to the students. The following are summaries of key components of our combined efforts.

Weekly self-evaluations

Much of our work throughout the early weeks of this project focused on trust building, team building, social skills needed for group work, and dynamics of the brainstorming process. These were all new concepts to the students, and the teachers weren't sure how to assess student progress in these areas. We ultimately decided to ask the students, and thus our weekly self-evaluations were born.

The format of the weekly self-evaluations solidified after a few weeks to include two sections. In the first, students rated themselves 1-10 on various aspects of their performance over the previous week. The content of these aspects or questions changed to meet the teachers' needs for feedback, but usually focused on social skills and classroom norms. The second section was for open-ended questions designed to facilitate student reflection on their learning and provide teachers with feedback on the individual needs of the students and information on the dynamics of the groups. This also proved to be a good opportunity for input on current issues by students who might not speak up in whole- group brainstorming sessions. Especially during the early going, some students were reluctant to speak up in whole-group sessions. A few never became completely comfortable with this. Since ideas and general information from weekly self-evaluations were shared anonymously with the whole class on a regular basis, this became another way for students to share comments and concerns and air ideas.

While most of the students immediately accepted the responsibility associated with self-assessment and reported very honestly, some had to test the system. The first week, several students gave themselves all "10s." The next day they discovered that evaluations with which teachers strongly disagreed resulted in private conferences where students were asked to defend their ratings. All of these students readily admitted they had not been honest and were glad to have the opportunity to redo their evaluations. The need for these conferences became very rare after the first couple of weeks. Interestingly, many conferences focused on students' rating themselves too low. Students who had not enjoyed a lot of success in school in the past often saw themselves unjustly deserving low grades. This was especially true of the special needs students (our group was inclusive) who initially saw themselves as not deserving of good grades, even though they were meeting all requirements and appropriate expectations.

For the students, these reports provided an opportunity for reflection and input. For teachers, this information became a focus for individual and group conferences and mini-lessons. Misunderstandings were often nipped in the bud because teachers were made aware of developing problems. Students took these weekly self-evaluations very seriously and decided they should be a factor in final grades. After being checked by teachers, these evaluations were included in students' portfolios and were shared with parents.

Reflective journals

Students reflected in journals at the end of each integrated studies block. They were expected to go beyond simply relating what they had done and were encouraged to think about their learning, how it related to previous learning, how it fit into future plans, and how they felt about their progress. This kind of activity was not something these students were familiar with. Quality reflection took coaching and facilitation, and many needed individual instruction and guidance. As it turned out, however, this became one of the areas where students displayed the greatest amount of growth.

Teachers usually scanned these journals each day and responded in them several times a week. They became a critical tool for promoting communications between students and teachers, as well as providing students with a real opportunity to practice personal writing skills.

Daily plans

Students began each integrated studies block by outlining and scheduling their plans for the day. Both group and individual time had to be scheduled. Originally this procedure was part of the students' journals.

FIGURE 2
Weekly Integrated Block Self-Evaluation

Name_____

<u>Rate yourself 1-10 on each item</u>

I got along well with others.	____
I did everything I was asked to do.	____
I respected other people and their property.	____
I used a 20-inch voice.	____
I stayed on task.	____
I listened when others were talking.	____
I didn't bother people when they were working.	____
I accomplished all the objectives for this week.	____
I put my goals and what I accomplished in my journal.	____
I filled out the bottom of this sheet thoughtfully.	____

This is what I learned in the integrated block this week (give examples):
_____
_____

Describe exactly what you did on your inquiry project this week. _____
_____
_____

Explain what each of the other members of your group contributed to your inquiry project._____
_____
_____

Describe in detail how you feel about the progress of your inquiry. _____

List what individual projects you worked on and what you did for each.
_____
_____

____ Ms. Mac & Mr. C agree with this report.
____ Ms. Mac & Mr. C disagree with a part of this report and would
     like to conference with you about it.

Please see Ms. Mac or Mr. C about a conference.

The process of checking these throughout the day, however, became unmanageable for teachers. Eventually it was decided that we needed a one-page form where students could briefly document plans, results, and questions each day. The form was designed so a week would fit on the two sides of a single sheet of paper. This made it much more convenient for teachers to check individual and group plans and determine if students were on task. Students who were off task were simply asked what they had agreed to do during that time period. This nearly always refocused them. It was received entirely differently than when teachers demanded that they get busy. Teachers could quickly scan the daily plans every day. The brief student reflections were developed further in their journals. These daily forms then become part of the students' working portfolios. An example of the daily planning sheet follows.

FIGURE 2
Daily Planning Sheet

Name: _____   Week of:_____

Monday
Goals (group and/or individual)_____

What I accomplished today:_____
_____

What I learned:_____
_____
_____

Resources used (in correct bibliographic form):_____
_____

Questions or concerns:_____
_____

Reflection is done in journal_____

Weekly conferences

Teachers conferred with individual students and groups at least weekly to document progress, discuss goals, offer suggestions, and work on problems. In some cases these conferences were more frequent, depending on the needs of students. At times they were even requested by students. Points of focus for these conferences often arose from the weekly self-evaluations.

Product assessments

By the time final products for the first theme began to materialize, these students were flying with the concept of self-assessment. It was as if they had known all along that they were the best judges of their own work, and it was about time someone asked them! With high interest and input from weekly self-evaluations, we went to whole- group brainstorming to discuss how their products would be assessed. Teachers maintained that the students must somehow display acquired knowledge. Students were equally adamant that effort should be rewarded. The questions then became: 1) Other than testing, which no one really wanted, how can you prove to teachers that you have gained new knowledge? 2) How can we measure effort? Exactly what could we see in a product that would indicate a lot of effort? This led to a frustrating discussion of criteria to demonstrate knowledge and effort. Finally a student raised his hand and said, "Neatness ... if I put in a lot of effort, it would be neat." "Yes!" I exclaimed, "wonderful!" At this point, the student thought he was really onto something until I continued, "What does neat look like?" and pushed him to really dig into specific criteria. While this was a difficult process, it was something we (the teachers) weren't going to abandon. In the end the investment of time turned out to be very worthwhile. The result of this work was a very usable assessment tool that belonged to the kids. Every criteria on the following rubric was generated by the students. These were the things they saw as important components of good work.

FIGURE 4
Product Assessment

Name _____ Name of Project _____

EFFORT	Poor	Fair	Good
Neatness (erasures, crumples, etc.)	___	___	___
Spelling	___	___	___
All requirements done	___	___	___
Relevance to theme	___	___	___
Creativity (something different)	___	___	___
Colorful	___	___	___
Details	___	___	___
KNOWLEDGE/ LEARNING			
Can answer oral question	___	___	___
Use of own words	___	___	___
Can use vocabulary words in sentences	___	___	___
Can explain illustrations presented by teaches	___	___	___
Can explain own illustrations and their relevance to the theme	___	___	___

Students determined the poor-fair-good ratings and decided how these would translate into letter grades; for instance, all goods was an A, all fairs a C, all poors a D-. Everyone agreed that if the assignment were done, even poorly, that the student shouldn't fail. It was decided that both individual students and teachers would assess the products using this student-generated checklist. The results of these assessments were compared, discussed, and negotiated at individual student/teacher conferences. If there were large discrepancies between the student's and teacher's assessments, both presented their case and compromised. After they agreed on what criteria were poor, fair, or good, a grade was determined. This part of the process might sound something like the teacher's saying, "We have 6 fairs, 4 goods, and 2 poors ... what do you think?" The students might reason, "Well, all fairs means a C, and I have more goods than poors ... what about a B-?" If acceptable to the teacher, the conference was over; if not, negotiations would continue. The students left these conferences not only knowing their grade, but also completely understanding why they got what they did. The grades had real meaning to them. Usually this process went very quickly as most student and teacher assessments were similar.

Presentation assessments

At the end of the theme, each group presented its inquiry project to the rest of the class. Since our product assessment tool did not fit the purposes of assessing oral presentations, we brainstormed new criteria. Once again this led to a workable, student-generated rubric (by now they were really getting the hang of this). The criteria were weighted as to what the students thought were the most important. They then decided that self, peer, and teacher assessments should all be factors of final presentation grades and that all peers would assess each presentation, providing an average for the peer portion of the grade. This turned out to be a wonderful idea, as it kept everyone focused. Students took this very seriously. Everyone was on task, and filling out the assessments provided a natural break between presentations. The comments they offered each other were helpful and interesting. The teachers' grades were averaged for their portion. It was decided that presenters should have the option of assessing themselves as a group or individually. All groups decided to do their assessment together and take a common grade. Students mandated two stipulations on this process that they saw as the teachers' responsibility. They said the teachers must challenge groups to defend their self-assessments, and that they must deal in some way with any peer assessments that seemed really off-the-wall, ones that might be much higher or much lower that anyone else's. Both of these situations turned up, but very rarely.

FIGURE 5
Presentation Assessment

PRESENTERS: _____

TOPIC: _____

EVALUATOR: _____

Had a lot of knowledge/information about their topic (30)   ___

Comments: _____

_____

Were able to answer questions about their topic (20)   ___

Comments: _____

_____

Everyone in the group participated in presentation (15)   ___

Comments: _____

_____

Visual aids were well prepared and relevant to topic (10)   ___

Comments: _____

_____

Communication:

Spoke clearly and understandably (5)   ___

Stayed on the subject (5)   ___

Used their own words (5)   ___

Talked to the class...didn't just read (5)   ___

Were polite answering questions (5)   ___

Comments: _____

_____

                                           TOTAL: ___

General comments about this presentation: _____

_____

_____

_____

Grade conferences

At the end of the quarter students presented their portfolios to the teaching team in individual conferences. Teachers inspected portfolios, discussed the students' averages, and asked questions appropriate to what students had done. Students proposed final grades for the quarter and were prepared to use their portfolios and related evidence to defend them. These grades were negotiated, and the students left the conferences with grades that were agreeable to everyone. Once again, students clearly understood where these grades were coming from.

Family conferences

Student/parent/teacher conferences were student directed, with students presenting their portfolios to their parents, sharing their grades, and explaining why they were getting these grades. They displayed work they were especially proud of, identified areas where they were struggling, and proposed goals for the next quarter to address these problems. These conferences were very well received by parents.

The sample evaluation tools included in this section are offered as examples of what sixth graders can do. It is important to stress that **these tools worked for us because they belonged to our students**. I would not recommend using them with another group. We certainly don't intend to. It is the process of developing these tools that is transferable. ♦

Integrative Block this year was neat and very interesting, because you got to find out things and learn different things every day.

The unit I liked best was the crime unit, because I got to see if crimes are increasing or decreasing, and compare how many murders, robberies, car thefts, and rapes happen each year. The second best unit was the environment. I liked that because I got to learn about animals and pollution. I also liked the future unit, because everyone got to see the different inventions everyone else thought of. I like the Integrative Block and the seventh graders should have it next year too, because it's fun!!!

The group work was fun because you got to work with other people that you didn't know about.

Helpful hints for the incoming sixth graders are: don't work with just your friends because you'll fool around, and get your work done so you'll get a good grade.

The thing I liked best about Integrative was more freedom because we had our choice of what we wanted to study and what we wanted to learn. I also like the daily and weekly evaluations. I liked the open houses and the food. I liked making decisions.

In group work, I learned not to work with people that talk and fool around all the time. I learned that working with groups is to cooperate, work together, and not waste time.

INCLUSION

SEPTEMBER						
		1	2	3	4
5	6	7	8	9	10	11
12	13	14	15	16	17	18
19	20	21	22	23	24	25
26	27	28	29	30		

Everyone flies first class on this ship

From day one of planning this project we felt that if this approach resulted in a good curriculum, it would be beneficial to all students. While the suggestion to include special needs students in the regular classroom came from the classroom teachers, it was immediately endorsed by the administration. The feelings were that these students gain more socially and intellectually from contact with their peers than they would in the isolation of the resource room. There is no special education in the real world. Sooner or later these kids will need to learn how to work with others.

To make this plan possible, the special education technician was assigned to work with these sixth-grade students full time in the regular classroom. While this teacher's primary responsibility was to assist the eight special needs students, the fact that she was in the classroom full-time proved to be a wonderful asset to the other students and the classroom teachers. Since the special needs students were spread out throughout several inquiry groups, this teacher ended up working with nearly everyone. She became useful in many areas including instruction, monitoring, assessment, and support. The fact that she worked with all students from time to time, made it look as if she were not singling out special needs students. Indeed, it was difficult for an outsider to tell which were the special needs students in these classes. This is extremely important, especially for this age group. Young adolescents desperately want to be part of the group. They all want to do what everyone else is doing. For some of these students, this was the first time in their school lives that they were truly part of the group. Self-esteem soared, and so did student achievement.

Instructionally, one of the keys to the success of the inclusion part of this experiment was making assignments open-ended enough for all students to take them to the limits of their abilities. Everyone did basically the same kinds of assignments, with different students working at different levels than others. Having the special education teacher to "download" instructions and other information for the special needs students was also critical. Just because these students were no longer in the resource room did not mean that they didn't still have special needs. These needs just had to be met within the context of the program in the regular classroom.

So as not to mislead readers into thinking the inclusion part of this project was easy, I need to acknowledge that there were severe difficulties and frustrations in the early going. Some of the special needs students were even more lacking in the social skills of cooperative work than the rest of the class. They also refused to believe we actually expected them to think and be responsible in any way for their learning. This had never been expected of them before. It was a major struggle to overcome the mind-set that teachers would give them all the information they would need and they would be happy as long as they did some busy work Eventually, however, they all came around and realized the satisfaction of doing the same things as everyone else. **The pride special needs students radiated while discussing their accomplishments was a thrill to see**. A couple of them actually became some of our best idea people and were highly respected in that capacity. These students were among those that showed the greatest amount of growth during this curriculum project.

The other students were amazingly tolerant of the special needs students. They accepted the fact that there were different expectations for individual students and tried to help the special needs students identify and expand on their strengths. In a state that is nearly homogeneous racially, this became a wonderful lesson on tolerance of diversity. ♦

This has been a good year in Integrative but it's one of the hardest classes you will ever have. At first group work was hard, but after you learned to get along with people and work together, it was easy.

At first I liked setting the classroom norms but then we had to make up consequences. Norms are like rules, nobody likes them but we have to have them to keep people straight.

This year I learned how to get information from the CD ROM and put it into my reports and how to do a lot of cool things on the computer, like charts and graphs.

At first I wasn't used to making decisions for myself. I was used to the teachers saying things like, 'Do all of page 174 in your text book,' instead of, 'What are you going to do today in class?' This way you learn responsibility and decision making.

Integrative is a class where all subjects are mixed together, like instead of just writing for the sake of writing, your writing is in reports and other things that go along with your projects.

I liked choosing partners, rules, and our topics. We weren't told what to do like usual. Things I learned were responsibility, debating, and reflecting on what I was learning. I learned other things too.

They should keep Integrative because it gave us skills we wouldn't learn otherwise. I didn't even know what a reflection was before. Now I do them every day. Integrative should be used in more schools.

THE CRIME UNIT

NOVEMBER						
	1	2	3	4	5	6
7	8	9	10	11	12	13
14	15	16	17	18	19	20
21	22	23	24	25	26	27
28	29	30				

Off we go into the wild blue yonder

As we began our second unit, the students took on even more responsibility, including selection of the theme. We started this process with students brainstorming in pairs and listing questions about their personal concerns. This took place as part of advisory sessions over several days. This was followed by listing students' questions about worldwide concerns. Armed with these lists, we moved to a whole-group session and compiled an extensive master list of questions about students' personal and world concerns. In a follow-up session, students were asked to study their lists of questions and identify major themes that encompassed overlapping questions from both of these lists. The following themes emerged:

Jobs/economy	War & Peace	Community/people
Pollution	Crime	Education
Future Environment	Space	Energy
Forests/Plants	Shelter	
Government	Health/Survival/Death	

And some say these kids aren't concerned about important issues! Their selections were all legitimate themes, certainly worthy of study by sixth graders and certainly enough to keep this team productively involved the rest of the year. The teachers readily saw how the traditional subject areas could easily be addressed within any of them.

The next step was to choose our second theme. We discussed possible issues that could be covered within each of these themes so students would have a general idea what they might be getting themselves into. We then voted, with students voting for as many themes as they wanted to. The ultimate selection was crime. The teachers immediately began to discuss possibilities for activities relevant to all content areas, science involved in recent innovations in crime detection, surveys and interviews, data to organize and graph, computer databases and spreadsheets to access and graph, job and career information, education related to these jobs, geography of states with various laws, lots of reading and writing, and obvious social implications.

Once the theme was selected, students brainstormed a list of exactly what they wanted to learn about crime and how they could pursue answers to these questions. New groups were formed, and group inquiry projects were proposed. Teachers, meanwhile, were working on givens they saw as appropriate to this theme. Student-generated activities, questions, and ideas were combined with teacher-generated givens, and through a collaborative effort of students and teachers, an action plan for this unit materialized. A time frame and deadlines were established, and we were flying again.

As expected, this unit unfolded more smoothly than the first. The work on self-assessment and classroom norms were all transferable as were the newly acquired skills related to computer use, writing process, finding and accessing resources, and working cooperatively.

The recent addition of a computer and Internet capability gave students access to e-mail and computer bulletin boards, and added new horizons to the resource situation. The students planned mini field trips, including visits to various crime prevention agencies.

FIGURE 6
Academic Givens for Crime Unit

The student will
- Work on information problem-solving by working together to locate, organize, and use information to produce meaningful products.
- Systematically collect, organize, and describe data.
- Construct, read, and interpret tables, charts, and graphs.
- Make inferences and convincing arguments that are based on data analysis.
- Write a business letter requesting information.
- Write a business letter thanking for information received.
- Be able to locate given states and countries.
- Investigate the science related to new innovations in crime detection.
- Read about the psychology of crime.
- Formulate and access computerized data bases and spreadsheets.
- Conduct research using sources other than standard library references.
- Compare and contrast statistics gathered.
- Review career possibilities in crime prevention and detection.

FIGURE 7
Crime Unit

Students will complete, but are not limited to, the following individual and group activities:

Individual

____ Business letter to assigned state requesting statistics.

____ Research and take part in a debate on an assigned topic.

____ Persuasive piece of writing on self-selected topic. Your opinions must be supported from readings and research you have done.

____ A bibliography of resources used in this unit. This includes readings, statistical data, letters from resources, etc.

____ Hand drawn chart or graph with a written narration of the information found on your chart/graph.

____ Complete all assigned readings with a short summary in your integrated journal.

Group

____ Develop a survey of at least 10 questions. Each group member will give the survey to 10 people. The data will be compiled individually and as a group.

____ Create a graph on the computer showing the information you collected from your group survey.

____ Contribute to the creation of a class database of crime statistics.

____ Group or Individual Inquiry—based on the "what we want to know about crime" list.

____ Letter to a foreign country asking for information on the class questions.

In response to a student invitation, an official from the Department of Juvenile Crime spent an afternoon at the school.

Meanwhile, the inquiry projects and related presentations were displaying much more variety and creativity, including integration of charts and graphs into presentations, attempts at writing and performing skits and plays, and a wonderful Crazy Crime Newspaper. The debates proved to be high points for the students. They discovered the necessity of doing research in order to identify different points of views on issues and enjoyed the challenge of presenting and defending outlooks that often differed from their own personal feelings.

Citizens from the community were once again the audience of choice. To share their work with adults, students organized another open house. To take advantage of the captive audience, they included a bake sale in order to raise funds for future field trips. This event was publicized in the local newspaper, and a good turnout resulted. Students presented their projects and information to a large group. Once again the night belonged to the students; they were wonderful hosts. The growth that had occurred over the first half of the school year was apparent to all. The success of these events added significantly to our community support. **The students were, without a doubt, the greatest promoters of the new curriculum.**

The way these sixth graders enthusiastically attacked this crime theme was more than sufficient payback for the time and frustrations it took to get them to this point. Students and teachers alike had attained a new level of comfort with the curriculum. Indeed, the curriculum had become truly organic and was generating its own energy.

An interesting aside occurred during the brainstorming sessions to identify themes. **All at once, students realized that they might not need student monitors any longer. Individuals were becoming responsible for their own behavior.** I remember clearly the day when, during yet another discussion of the problems of peer monitoring, a student raised his hand and said, "We all know the rules, right?" To which the rest of the class responded, "Well I should think so...we wrote them and we've been talking about them for weeks!" The young man then declared, "Well if we all know the rules, maybe we don't need monitors at all. Why can't we each monitor our own behavior?" What a concept!! I excitedly inquired, "Could you really do that? Could all of you do that? Is there anyone who thinks he or she couldn't do that?" By this time they were committed to making it work, and for the rest of the year this is exactly what happened. Sometimes someone would slip up and was reminded of the norms by the whole group, but mostly individuals monitored themselves and behaved in a manner acceptable to the group.

We, the teachers, had talked about this as an ultimate goal, but never actually expected to see it happen. I cannot overemphasize my feelings on this matter. If we want students to behave responsibly, we must give them opportunities to practice responsible behavior. As long as we continue to make and enforce all the rules for them, we will never see the behavior we want. I have come to believe that early adolescents will behave the way you expect them to. If you treat them like you expect them to do something irresponsible, they usually comply—as soon as they get a chance. If you let them know they are trusted and expected to act responsibly, they usually respond with responsible behavior. These sixth graders reinforced this belief for me. ♦

EXPANDING THE
INTEGRATED BLOCK

JANUARY						
						1
2	3	4	5	6	7	8
9	10	11	12	13	14	15
16	17	18	19	20	21	22
23	24	25	26	27	28	29
30	31					

Adjusting to weightlessness

A few weeks into the crime unit, students started asking for more time to work on thematic units. There was so much more they wanted to do, and they were becoming frustrated with scheduling around pull-outs. Integrated studies activities started to flow into the other blocks, especially the reading and writing. The teachers were also interested in expanding the integrated studies block, as well as moving it into the morning to give it more of a "prime time" emphasis. We wanted to send the message that this was what we thought was most important, that this was the "real stuff," not just an "add-on." These issues sent us into a full-blown discussion of how to revise the sixth-grade schedule. One of the big advantages of the organizational structure in this school is that teams have ultimate flexibility and freedom to adjust schedules. Except for lunch, physical education, and music once a week, teams are free to schedule their time as they see fit.

Much of the teachers' discussion about the new schedule centered on integrating what had been content area "givens" into the thematic units. The literacy piece was easy. All reading and writing givens were easily adapted to the integrated format. There was no compromise of literacy expectations. In fact, these students ended up exceeding the accomplishments of previous years in these areas. Most social studies givens also transferred quite easily. Math, however, was another story. While there was certainly lots of great math going on within the thematic units, teachers were reluctant to abandon the sequential progression of math skills that seemed to be expected (this seems to be a common area of concern across the nation when moving toward integrated curriculum and has become an area of fascination for me personally).

Other issues that played into the planning of the new schedule were ways of attaining more accessibility to computers and library resources and building in an opportunity to receive extra help to complete assignments for those students who needed it. There was no study hall in the original schedule, and the busing situation in this school district makes after-school assistance impossible.

The structure of our new schedule quickly materialized. It was decided that mid-year would be a logical time for this transition, although all, especially the kids, were ready for it considerably before this point. The new schedule looked like this:

    30 minutes - Advisory
    60 minutes - Math
    150 minutes - Integrated Studies
            Lunch
    20 minutes - Read-Aloud
    50 minutes - Mini-Courses
    50 minutes - Study Lab/Activity Period

Themes being addressed within the integrated studies units still infiltrated other blocks. Activities related to these units often flowed into advisory and math. Books for read-aloud were often chosen to reinforce the theme. Mini-courses were usually offshoots of the integrated studies, but could also be used to cover curriculum givens that didn't easily fit into chosen themes (for example, this block was used to read *Johnny Tremain* to meet a Revolutionary period social studies given). At times, when all the pieces were falling in place, this schedule took on the appearance of a totally integrated day.

The revised schedule met our needs very nicely. The students had time to pursue their interests in depth, and the emphasis of the school day clearly became focused on the thematic units. **However scheduled, it must be clear that integrated studies are central in the curriculum, not just an addition to the existing program.** ♦

I liked doing the studies and making projects to show what we learned about our topic. I liked having all the open houses, being able to show something about what we learned, and presenting. We got to look into those things we found most interesting.

I liked being able to give my opinions about my education. I think it makes it more fun. I liked brainstorming and picking our topics. I especially liked having a say in my grades.

I didn't really like all the assignments, but it did make you work harder. All the reflections sometimes got boring.

We had a lot of decisions to make on our education. We learned how to look up stuff that we didn't know how to find before. I like the rules because we made them and we abided by them. It was fun to find out stuff on your own and to try to answer your own questions.

Integrative was so cool because we got to sign out and didn't have to ask the teacher to go to the computers or to the library. We could work in groups and we could pick them ourselves, or we could work alone. We studied recycling, future inventions, crime rates, and how we are going to survive. Groups decided their own projects.

We decided when to do homework and make-up work.

I think we should have integrative next year because it's fun and you can really learn about the world and what we can do to help the world.

THE FUTURE UNIT

MARCH					
	1	2	3	4	5
6	7	8	9	10	11	12
13	14	15	16	17	18	19
20	21	22	23	24	25	26
27	28	29	30			

Settling into orbit

The future...what a wide-open theme! Everyone saw this as an opportunity to be really creative. Students were anxious to develop ideas about what they thought things would look like in 50 years. Teachers, to keep these activities from becoming exercises in fantasy writing, required that all predictions be based on research of the past and present. This actually worked very well and led to some interesting historical inquiries as well as fascinating, scientifically based, future predictions.

Students started by brainstorming questions and activities that might be appropriate as means for pursuing answers to these questions. Teachers studied their givens and collaborated with students to formulate an action plan (p. 46) for their study of the future.

New inquiry groups formed, and group proposals were prepared and presented to teachers. Groups chose some aspect of community life to work on, researched the past and presented status of their topic, and used the information to make informed predictions of the future. They prepared displays to help present their information to the class.

Future Unit Requirements

The Future Unit will run from Monday, February 28, to Friday, April 1st. There will be due dates on certain requirements, others will be due at the end of the unit. There will be group and individual requirements as usual. If you are doing your future project as an individual, you have the same requirements as the groups.

Individual Requirements:
— Writing: Each of the assigned pieces must be at least two pages in rough draft form. They must go through the complete writing process (brainstorm, web, two conferences, editor checklist, turn in to Ms. Mc and conference with her, publish on computer, publisher's checklist).
Conversation must be used **correctly** in at least one piece.
__ First person writing (me, I, we, us, etc.). Final copy due_____
__ Third person writing (they, them, he, etc.). Final copy due____
__ Conversation is used correctly
__ Future vocabulary log (words on back of this paper)
__ Bibliography of all resources used (in correct form)
__ Read assigned articles and summarize them in your journal by assigned date

Group Requirements:
__ Article for future class newsletter
__ Future inquiry project: This future forecast will be based on research from past and present. Students must be able to show what they based their forecast on and where they got the information.
__ Inventions make the future bright.
  1) Figure out a problem your group wants to solve and explain it.
  2) Describe your unique invention and how it works (illustrations would be good here).

The variety of the presentations demonstrated considerable growth when compared to the first unit last fall. We were treated to a wonderfully creative live fashion show displaying past, present, and future clothes. The young women in this group utilized a wide variety of research methods, as well as important life skills. Displays of models of past, present, and future household appliances and methods of transportation were prepared by other groups. One group studied the history of space travel and predicted how future generations could live in space.

A prediction of what education would look like in the future put on by one group included trips to old school buildings in the area. In some cases this involved study of the remains of the foundations of buildings to see how they were laid out. It was interesting that the students' predictions were in the direction of the smaller schools of the past and away from the conglomerate model of the present. A study of shelters resulted in an intricate, well-constructed model of a future house that incorporated numerous innovations. In a study of war, a group predicted what future weaponry might look like. Unfortunately they didn't consider the possibility of a future without war. Presumably our emphasis on basing predictions on past and present events prevented this from being considered as an option.

Another outstanding project predicted the physical outlook of a local community. This work was based on research trips to the public library, interviews, and an accumulation of wonderful, historic pictures. Looking to the community as a resource—which had seemed so foreign to these students just a few months ago—now seemed completely natural. **Students were readily integrating a wide variety of research skills in their investigations.** The intricacies of working cooperatively and learning from peers were becoming second nature. They were cruising under their own power, with teachers nudging, coaching, facilitating, guiding, and encouraging.

An interesting sideline of this unit grew out of the invention piece. The assignment was for groups to identify a problem and design an invention to deal with it. This proved to be engaging for the students and led to some high levels of thinking. The interesting part, however, resulted from an exploration of the Internet, which turned up a Canadian middle school working on a similar project. This led to our students' telecommunicating with young people from another country. Suddenly this new technology, which we had been experimenting with for just a few weeks, became very relevant. Some students became very adept at telecommunication skills. In fact, they bypassed the limited knowledge of the teaching staff and became the "experts" for the school.

These young adolescents were mastering and displaying skills that went far beyond the accumulation of information. By this point in the year, even after the slow start, they had exceeded our most optimistic expectations. This might be a good place to reemphasize the need to give curriculum change time to evolve. If we had not been so determined to make it work, it would have been very easy to abandon this project within the first several weeks. There were certainly enough stress inducers and frustrations during the initial phases to have warranted it. It is important to point out, however, that once the students got the feel of what we hoped for them and understood our commitment to their full involvement, they took off and covered much more ground than they ever would have under the old curriculum procedures. ◆

THE SURVIVAL UNIT

APRIL						
			1	2	3	4
5	6	7	8	9	10	11
12	13	14	15	16	17	18
19	20	21	22	23	24	25
26	27	28	29	30		

Time for the big payoff

The final unit of the year, survival, coincided nicely with student interests, teacher givens, and the chance to get outside and take advantage of some wonderful spring weather. Students had many questions related to both health issues and survival techniques. In previous years, the teachers had enjoyed teaching CPR and water safety. These interests very easily fell into place and resulted in the action plan on the next page.

During this unit we saw skills really come together. It was no longer necessary to assign things like interviews, surveys, or letter writing. These techniques had become natural options for these students. **At times the whole day became completely integrated.** Popular survival books were chosen for read-aloud, and students rotated through mini-courses on CPR and orienteering. Community support for teaching CPR and water safety was overwhelming. After a long Maine winter, kids and teachers alike were ready to get outside. The stage was set for some marvelous learning experiences that also turned out to be pure fun.

FIGURE 9
Requirements for Survival Unit

Individual Requirements

___ Health research paper and poster project – 3 page hand-written rough draft of paper sent through the writing process and published on the computer.

___ 1-2 page final reflection on learning and skills gained during the integrated block.

___ DARE reflection

___ Demonstrate ability to perform aid for a choking victim, rescue breathing, and CPR on an infant and child.

___ Demonstrate knowledge of safety and first aid procedures.

___ Demonstrate basic knowledge of water safety and rescue techniques.

___ Assigned readings from *READ* magazine and discussions on those readings.

___ Be able to orally give directions from the school to home, giving road names and route numbers.

___ Be able to read a road map and topographic map and identify different landmarks.

___ Be able to use a compass by reading it in degrees (outside).

___ Make a survival kit.

___ Have knowledge of basic survival skills to use in case of emergencies.

Group Requirements

___ An inquiry to explore one of the types of survival brainstormed by the class.

Probably the most significant piece of student work unfolded from this unit. As an inquiry project, a group of four young women decided to study how the homeless survive. Even though homeless people are uncommon in our rural setting, they were aware that homelessness was a growing problem in nearby Bangor, Maine, 60 miles away. How to approach these unfortunate people posed an interesting predicament. After conversing with area television stations, however, our students were put in contact with The Greater Bangor Area Homeless Shelter. They communicated with the director of this facility by mail and phone then planned their first trip to the shelter. At the shelter they interviewed many of the homeless persons and produced a videotape.

Some of the comments they shared with us upon their return follow:

She (the director) told us when people come in she doesn't look at their race, background, record, or what they look like.

When they come in she has them sign a card that has the rules on the back.

They can stay as long as they want if they follow the rules and look for a job and a regular place to stay.

Everyone thinks that homeless people are criminals and bad people but they are people just like us and really nice.

Upon their return home, these young women knew they wanted to do something to assist these needy people. They decided to organize a food and clothing drive. In their words, "We collected at least 30 boxes of food and clothing. Then we brought it down to them. They really liked the warm clothes and food." The genuine caring displayed by these girls spread throughout the class. Everyone felt connected to this project. There were few dry eyes in the room during their presentation as they related their contact with a pregnant fourteen-year-old homeless girl at the shelter. A "big city" problem had come home for this group of young adolescents in rural Maine. Talk about community service! And what about tolerance of diversity; could any teacher-generated projects have even approached the effectiveness of this experience? Not likely.

Other inquiry projects and presentations included desert survival, forest survival, interesting ways of getting water, surviving in the snow, a wonderful display of edible native wild plants, and creative ways to make fish hooks, traps, and weapons.

Health reports were outstanding and demonstrated a wide variety of research skills. This was an assignment that had been done by sixth-grade students in previous years, but it was interesting to see how this group took this assignment to a much higher level. This provided a rare point of reference for the teachers and confirmed what we felt intuitively—student-oriented curriculum translates into more effective learning.

Other high points of this unit included a class trip to the ocean where students demonstrated their survival kits and tested their skills at building fires from scratch in the rain no less. This trip also included lessons on ocean survival and marine life by our local expert who happened to be a school board member. Another field trip took the entire class to a college swimming pool to test water safety skills. ♦

The best thing about Integrative was that it saved us from just doing work in textbooks. Another good thing was the topics we did. My favorite was endangered species. I liked doing our picture book.

I think the best thing about Integrative Block this year was how the whole sixth grade got to choose together what we were going to be able to study. We studied crime, environment, future, and even survival. That was fun because we got to make survival kits and learned how to save lives.

When I found out we were going to be making our own decisions, I was very happy because I had never done that in school before.

I learned how to use the computer and to make graphs. I also learned how to choose the right people to work with. It was fun when we made our own consequences, but everyone was a little hard on themselves and each other.

Some people in the school thought we weren't learning anything. WRONG!! We had to find all the information on what we were studying. We were the ones who had to do projects and do vocabulary logs, read, design inventions, do lots of writing, learn about computers, and whatever else you or your group planned. We had to study the past to predict the future or if there was going to be a future.

Integrative was fun. It was something new for all of us. When we first came to school I expected it to be the same, like books, papers, etc. But we started a whole new thing and everything was different. It was more fun and a lot more exciting.

What I liked most about Integrative was the presentations and grading the other kids and ourselves. It wasn't just the teachers grading, it was us too.

I liked how we got to make rules.

I learned a lot of things like how to use the computers and especially about life saving and the Heimlich maneuver.

The classroom norms worked well because we all cooperated.

I liked how we got to pick our own groups and could work on what we wanted to when we wanted to. I wouldn't change anything because it all went so smooth this year.

The thing I liked best was doing the group projects. I liked making my own decisions.

I learned how to use the CDROM and the index in an encyclopedia.

In groups I learned to share the work that had to be done.

The best thing about Integrative is you learn a lot. I think you learn much better if you decide what to learn, not a teacher giving you a textbook and worksheets to keep you busy.

LESSONS LEARNED

SEPTEMBER						
JUNE						
			1	2	3	4
5	6	7	8	9	10	11
12	13	14	15	16	17	18
19	20	21	22	23	24	25
26	27	28	29	30		

What experience taught us

Although the project described in this book was limited to one year in one school, we believe the lessons derived from our experiences are valid. They can serve as guides and provide encouragement to others who seek to make school more effective and vital.

1) **The power of ownership should never be underestimated.**

   Rules, curriculum, content, and assessment measures take on new meaning when they belong to you. This point was driven home time and time again as we interacted with these sixth graders. It was an incredibly refreshing experience to work with kids who were enthused about what they were doing. Their growth in academic achievement, behavior, and willingness to take responsibility for their own learning was inspiring. They exceeded our expectations in all areas, primarily because of the fact, we are convinced, that they saw what they were doing as "theirs."

2) **Young adolescents want desperately to do "real" work, things that have meaning for them and significance in their community.**

   They are capable of much more responsible, intellectual, and socially acceptable endeavors than they have traditionally been given credit for. We found that these sixth graders had very significant and legitimate concerns about themselves and the world around them. They are interested in important issues, not just in drivel as their stereotype indicates. The list of themes generated by these sixth graders illustrates their seriousness. Once they acquired ownership of the themes and were actively involved in developing related activities, they readily accepted teacher givens. When curriculum planning becomes a collaborative effort, everyone wins. Students acquire ownership, and teachers have excited and engaged kids to guide.

3) **Traditional content can be incorporated within a student-oriented curriculum.**

   In most areas we found that these sixth graders met or exceeded the content learning of previous classes. Some of what they learned arose from student inquiries and some from teacher givens. The big bonus was all the other learning that took place simultaneously. Never before had these students attained such high levels of social, communicative, and cooperative skills. Never before had they learned the lessons of time management, accepted responsibility for locating resources, or monitored their own behavior. Never had they demonstrated such high levels of critical thinking skills. Never had the school-community connection been so strong. And these lessons were not learned at the expense of "traditional content." In fact we believe the level of understanding of that content exceeded previous levels due to the enthusiasm and engagement of the students.

4) There is no need to fear student empowerment.

Our experience with sixth graders indicates that young adolescents respond very positively to empowerment. They are fully capable of making many types of choices and decisions. In fact, they thrive on it! Empowerment is contagious. Once the seeds germinate, the growth is rapid and healthy. When it finally sank in that we were actually going to take their suggestions and ideas seriously, these young people flourished. They soon sought involvement in every aspect of their school lives. The hard part was overcoming our own fears and the mind-set of students that had developed from years of passivity. There's no turning back, however—once you involve them in decision making, be prepared to live with their choices.

5) Young adolescents become very reflective when they are provided time and encouragement to think about their learning.

The quality of students' reflections, both written and oral, improved remarkably. While they struggled with this at first, they eventually grew to enjoy revisiting and rethinking what they had learned and done. This helped them become much better at applying their learning to new situations. Daily reflection became part of the regular program. They no longer saw it as a separate assignment they had to complete but as an important part of their learning.

Reflection is critical to learning and self-assessment. Unfortunately, it does not happen spontaneously. It must be initiated and nourished. It takes time to develop and maintain, but the results are worth it. Reflection is a condition that we must model in a variety of ways so it will become ingrained as a part of the learning process.

6) Young adolescents are quite capable of assessing their own work.

They have an intuitive sense of what constitutes good work and with a little coaching, will identify important criteria. They are inherently honest and become very critical when assessing themselves. They greatly appreciate knowing the criteria by which they are being judged. When they develop such criteria, that takes on even more significance. If we accept the concept of students' taking on responsibility for their own learning, we must help them articulate what quality work looks like and help them to assess their own work against the criteria they developed.

7) When given the chance, young adolescents are able to show what they have learned in creative ways.

There are many ways to demonstrate learning. While traditional tests may do an adequate job of showing what students don't know, they are a very narrowly focused measure of what has been learned. One goal was to allow students to discover and build on their strengths. When provided opportunities, students creatively found ways to demonstrate what they had learned. This is not to say that they had completely free reign in this area. Journals, reflections, reports, presentations, and portfolios were required, still leaving a lot of latitude for creatively demonstrating personal learning.

Students were slow getting started in this area. Their backgrounds had offered limited experiences in assessing school work. Most of the original products they chose took the form of models and papers. As the year progressed, however, the variety of products expanded to include videos, dramatic productions, debates, artwork, fashions, graphs, charts, newspapers, and other products. Individuals had freedom to use their particular strengths and interests to demonstrate evidence of their learning.

8) Young people are capable of responsible behavior.

One of the most striking results we witnessed was in the area of student behavior. We saw an evolution from relative chaos to students who developed their own classroom norms, from teachers who had to control every aspect of student behavior to students who could monitor their own actions, creating a true cooperative community.

Students respond to a show of trust and usually act the way they are expected to. They know rules are necessary and have a keen sense of what is right and fair. We found them fully competent of making their own rules and consequences and monitoring their own behavior. They pay a lot more attention to rules that belong to them. The behavior modeled by these sixth graders in the classrooms transferred to other areas of the school. Their mutual respect, responsible behavior, and tolerance of diversity were observable in many situations. Teachers' high expectations in this area were very clear. The message the students received was that they were respected and trusted, and it was assumed that they would act responsibly. And that is exactly what they did. Young people respond with the type of behavior that is expected of them.

9) Given trust and a sense of community, young adolescents will open up and express themselves.

As the year progressed it was interesting to see how much more freely and ably these young people expressed their ideas and opinions. A true sense of community developed. All students came to feel they could say what they wanted without fear of ridicule. Once ground rules were established and students became comfortable, they did very well in small- and large-group brainstorming sessions. We regularly convened 40 sixth graders in a regular classroom. Communication during these whole-group sessions became free and open. All opinions were respected. Everyone listened to what was being said. Individuals had developed a sense of how they wanted the group to respond when it was their turn to talk or present, and then transferred this image to guide their own behavior. They sensed that special consideration was needed with so many people in such a small space.

10) Having an audience beyond the teacher is critical.

If students are going to see their studies as having real importance, they need to have an audience beyond the teacher with whom to share their work. This audience can be comprised of classmates, other students and teachers, parents, or community citizens. The audience should be composed of persons the students want to engage and impress. The choice of audience, where possible, should be theirs. The role of the audience is primarily to affirm to the students that their work is important and worth doing.

11) The community can provide abundant resources to enrich the school's program.

All communities, even small, rural ones, have valuable educational resources. They may take forms other than traditional literary sources, but they are there. These young people had developed a real capacity for locating and accessing community resources. They wrote to, called, and interviewed a great number of people in search of information. It was difficult at first to guide them toward looking beyond textbooks to locate sources of information, but they found it interesting and exciting after they got started. They enticed many parents and other community members into contributing to their projects in a variety of ways. They also drew on the community as an audience for sharing their work. The resulting flow of students into the community, and the community into the school, was refreshing and went a long way toward building widespread community support. Most importantly, students saw their work as "real" when it involved community people. We didn't have to contrive relevance. The community became responsive and more supportive. The reaction of everyone involved was overwhelmingly positive.

12) The two-teacher team organization promotes integration of curriculum.

Traditional middle school teams are composed of four or five subject-area teachers. This condition nearly always reinforces the practice of keeping these areas separate most of the time. As long as teachers are responsible for teaching a single content area, in equal time slots, attempts at integrative curriculum often only result in short-term, ineffective, multidisciplinary units that demonstrate forced relationships and require enormous amounts of planning time (Bishop & Allen-Malley, 2004). What is advocated here is organizing around partnerships of teaching generalists. This permits true "team teaching," with the flexibility to group students and teachers in a wide variety of ways and concentrate the instruction of content and skills needed by the students to do the particular task at hand. This team structure offers the ultimate in flexibility and also addresses several other components of the middle school concept (Alexander, 1993), including the need for students to form close relationships with adults in the school. With 40 to 50 students spending the bulk of their school day with just two teachers, these relationships evolve naturally. Advisory-type activities are easily integrated within the ongoing program as well.

13) All students do not immediately embrace this approach to developing curriculum.

No curriculum plan or approach has yet been identified that works for all students at all times. Especially during initial implementation, we witnessed some student resistance. To a large extent, this resistance came from students who had been very successful with the traditional curriculum while expending a minimum of effort. Some students who were good at memorizing and taking tests didn't see why they should have to make decisions and actually "think." They had been getting "As" for years without thinking, why change? Some of the "best students" were displaced by others who struggle in more traditional classrooms. The transition was not an easy one for some. With very few exceptions, however, everyone eventually came around. Student reflections at the end of the year indicated nearly universal approval of our curriculum. In these reflections, some of which have been scattered throughout these pages, it was interesting to see how they frequently used words like "we" and "ours" when referring to the curriculum.

14) Conscious effort is needed to maintain focus on your long-term goals.

When problems developed, the natural instinct was to pound our fists on the table and lay down the law. But would this have done anything toward achieving our goal of teaching our students to solve real-life problems? Would that have taught them to become responsible for their own behavior? Wouldn't we be letting them off too easily if we solved the problem for them? We had to keep reminding ourselves, and each other, of these issues and of the plan to take problems back to the students. Eventually it began to feel more natural to do this. The usual procedure called for bringing the whole class together and presenting them with the problem. "Here it is, guys. This isn't working, and we can't live with it. What are we going to do about it?" Resulting solutions were often simpler and more appropriate than anything we (as teachers) had thought of. Our students had wonderful problem-solving experiences, took on more responsibility, and usually adhered to resulting rules because each of these opportunities belonged to them.

15) A student-centered curriculum is demanding yet rewarding.

In the beginning, be prepared for long hours of planning, initial resistance from students who have mastered passivity, high levels of stress, frustrations, and even failures. But also be prepared for eventual success, real gratification, and exhilarating classroom experiences more interesting and enjoyable than you thought possible. Every day in school will be different, just as every student's needs are different. Be prepared to take on new and different roles. The fact that the teacher is, to some extent, liberated from the role of "information giver," does not mean free time, but it does provide new satisfactions as the teacher assumes the roles of facilitator, coach, collaborator, and guide.

16) A student-centered curriculum requires adequate preparation and knowledge of oneself.

Because a student-centered curriculum is such a major departure from traditional practice it demands much of the teacher. It is essential that the teacher have self-confidence, patience, and even a thick skin. Your colleagues may not all see you in a positive light. Having a well-articulated and active philosophy of education and a set of beliefs about learning and kids is essential along with being secure in your personhood.

Beyond that it is important that you be well read in contemporary middle school curriculum. Read Beane (1993; 2005), Stevenson and Carr (1993), Springer (1994; 2006), and Brazee and Capelluti (1995), among others to immerse yourself in the concepts, ideas, and successful examples of integrated studies—and to gain encouragement. And recognize too that you, while risking, are riding the wave of the future in middle level education.

What lies ahead?

What is going to happen when these kids bring their sixth-grade experience to the seventh grade—and beyond—and a much more traditional setting? We can only speculate at this time. Certainly the students are going to deliver a message about the power of ownership to their future teachers. Whether anyone listens remains to be seen. No matter what happens in the future, however, their experiences with their student-oriented curriculum year can never be taken away from them. They developed skills that will remain with them for the rest of their lives. I would hope they speak out against the inevitable return to being passive receivers of information; but they will have to take what comes. We spent some time near the end of the year preparing these upcoming seventh graders for this transition, mostly with discussions of the need to be aware that different teachers would have different expectations of them and employ their own methods. Actually, they were very aware of this already. Our expectations were certainly different than any they had confronted up to this point. The big problem is that even though they have extensive prior experience as passive learners now they know how it feels to "fly;" so I hope a "crash landing" is not inevitable. ♦

EPILOGUE

JANUARY 2006						
1	2	3	4	5	6	7
8	9	10	11	12	13	14
15	16	17	18	19	20	21
22	23	24	25	26	27	28
29	30	31				

Reflections
12 years later

Wallace Alexander

It has been 12 years since these experiences with student-oriented curriculum first took place. All involved have grown, matured, and moved on in their personal journeys. As Kathy McAvoy and Dennis Carr continued their program, it became a model for hundreds of teachers and teams; and the original book became an important professional development tool in schools across the country. Its messages inspired many who moved to develop some form of curriculum integration. We all knew we were involved in something important. You will read more about Kathy and Dennis in their reflections that follow.

For me, my journey the next year took me to another small, rural school in Sedgwick, Maine, where I worked on a partner team with Phil Cotty, one of the most student-oriented teachers I have ever known. From there I moved to the University of Maine to complete an Ed.D. degree that included a dissertation focusing on teams who were transitioning to thematic, student-oriented curriculum. I have continued to work with teachers, presenting and consulting at conferences and institutes...working with some of the most incredible and progressive educators in the U.S. My journey has been a satisfying one.

But what of those young adolescents whose names are included in this book? I wish I could tell you that we have 12 years of detailed data on their successes. We don't. Any follow-ups were sporadic and anecdotal. I would like to tell you that each and every child accomplished impressive intellectual feats. Some did. Some didn't. I'm quite certain that all graduated from high school. One was, indeed, valedictorian. Others struggled. Some went to college. Some didn't. A few went to war. Their academic and vocational patterns were much like those of other sixth graders who moved through Mount Jefferson. But I am convinced there were lasting differences.

I've seen many of these now young adults throughout the past 12 years. I've seen some of them at high school ball games. I've seen some during their college years, at their jobs, in airports, in stores, and in various other everyday places. Recently, I've even bumped into a couple who were new teachers.

Here are some of the things I find special and different about these students. I've never encountered any of these people when they didn't seek me out to speak to me. Not once. If they had others with them, they would introduce me and often mention that I'm the guy who wrote the book about them. And in nearly every case, they have initiated a discussion of their sixth-grade year, recalling where this or that happened in great detail. They remember the units of study, the authentic work, and the skills they learned to accomplish that work. But even as delightful and gratifying as these discussions are, they often mentioned things even more significant. They talk of things they learned that they didn't realize they learned until later in life. They mention feelings of independence, collegiality, and inspiration. Their tone is one of fondness. Yes, we made lasting differences in the lives of these sixth graders, ones that do not happen enough in our schools.

Dennis Carr

Reflecting on the student-oriented or democratic curriculum twelve years later, I still believe this approach is far better for students than the more traditional, teacher-directed curriculum. An integrative approach gives students' ownership in how they learn the "established curriculum" set for them by state guidelines, such as Maine's *Learning Results*, specific grade level expectations, and the requirements of No Child Left Behind. Such mandates have caused teachers and administrators to believe they must abandon the creativity of student-oriented curriculum to prepare their students to meet the criteria of high stakes tests. Not so!

Experts in the business world tell us that schools need to do a much better job teaching "people skills." This curriculum does that. I observed our students learning skills in ways I had never seen before. I've also seen these students not only meeting the requirements of the old curriculum but also mastering many other skills that can't be measured by testing. These sixth graders sent business letters all over the country and received responses answering their questions. They made countless phone calls, went into the community to conduct interviews, organized small-group field trips, arranged for their own transportation needs, selected their own groups to work with on cooperative projects, and much more. Possibly the greatest strength of this program was that students had ownership in what they were doing because the curriculum evolves from their own interests and concerns. This brought the quality of student work to a much higher level. The vast majority of students liked this approach to curriculum and instruction much better than the textbook-lecture-test model. This was the first time our students had ever expressed interest in what they thought was important.

To determine the effects of our integrated curriculum approach as measured by standardized tests, I analyzed the test results for the first three years of the student-oriented program for students in grades five through seven at our school. At that time our school district used the

Iowa Test of Basic Skills to assess student growth. The data showed that over a three-year period, the sixth-grade integrated classroom had a significant increase in the number of students scoring in the high range on these tests, compared to students in the more traditional classroom. We also noted that students showed a tendency to regress on all Iowa subtests, once they returned to a more traditional classroom in the seventh grade.

I also looked at the test results for years four and five of the program. Kathy McAvoy, my teaching partner for nine years in the integrated program, had moved to a new position. Because she was replaced with a first-year teacher with no experience in teaching, no experience working on a two-person team, and no experience working in an integrative classroom, we scaled back the integrative program. This meant more of a traditional classroom in the morning with the integrative program in the afternoon. Even with this abbreviated program, the test results were similar as the Iowa test scores held strong, with the sixth grade placing more students in the high range and fewer in the low range compared to the fifth and seventh grade classroom's traditional structures.

Much as one test does not fit every student, one instructional approach does not meet the varied learning needs of all young adolescents. In order to develop these skills I believe the integrative approach is superior to the "stand-up lecture and read your textbook model." I have witnessed the effort—and abilities—of middle level students as learning styles grow significantly when working in an integrative curriculum and using cooperative groups. I must admit that curriculum integration involved much more work, but it was well worth it.

But, what does it take to have a successful student-oriented classroom? First, you must have a team of teachers committed to the same goals for the program. Team members must be willing to bypass their "comfort zones" and push themselves to provide rigorous and relevant units designed for and by their students. They must be committed to such a program and understand why such a program is better for young adolescents, not just that it works.

The next most important ingredient is the support of the administration. Administrators must be familiar with the various facets and nuances of integrative curriculum. We can help educate administrators by inviting them to attend workshops to learn what to expect when they enter an integrative classroom. They should also observe students brainstorming critical issues, solving problems, and analyzing issues across content areas. Without administrative and parental support no program will be successful.

Now, as a school principal, I find it very difficult to continue and maintain the giant leaps toward curriculum integration Kathy McAvoy and I achieved in the first years of our program. Teachers and school boards are now totally focused on preparing students for the next assessment test. With all the other mandates on teachers today to develop their own local assessment systems, ensuring all students are working to meet standards, fewer teachers have the energy or will to undertake the challenge of developing a program where student voice and democratic participation are at the forefront.

To new as well as veteran teachers interested in curriculum integration, my advice remains the same: "Just do it." Plant the seed and start it growing. Involve parents who want their children to be able learners and safe at school. The integrative approach will help their children learn the information necessary to meet the standards and develop the skills and learning strategies necessary for the real world.

One final caveat: This type of curriculum is not something you can package as a one-model fits all. While units with similar themes may reappear each year, how students meet the objectives each year and what they learn will be different as the needs, skills, and concerns of the current students are taken into account. Any changes to the teaching team may make the process entirely different as well.

My convictions about our student-oriented curriculum remain strong. Our students accomplished much; they met the standards but developed their own work habits at the same time. They found meaning in their work in the essential questions they posed and answered, the research they undertook, and the projects they produced.

Kathy McAvoy

It has been more than a dozen years since Dennis Carr and I started on our journey into integrative curriculum. I have always labeled the experience of developing curriculum with students as the "best of the best" of my teaching career. Early on I knew I would never go back to the traditional way of teaching I had followed, even though my teaching style has never been considered "traditional" by many people. I'm convinced that the changes we made to facilitate an integrative curriculum were for the better—both for our students and for ourselves as professionals.

My commitment to a student-oriented curriculum became much stronger over the years as I saw the quality and quantity of time I spent with my students. Before, I was the "knowledge giver" making sure my students *received* all the "knowledge" I thought they should acquire. Later, I saw myself learning along with the students and becoming more of a facilitator, guide, and coach. I had so much more quality one-on-one contact with every one of my students when we implemented integrative curriculum.

Another highlight of our student-oriented curriculum was that our parents were much more involved. Whenever we started a new unit, a newsletter went out asking for help, resources, and ideas from parents, families, and community members. We always received offers of speakers willing to share expertise, books and magazines, and drivers for field trips. In these ways parents took an active part in what their children were doing in school. Most communications sent home required a signature to be returned to school. That let us know that parents received the information we sent them. One parent told us, "I've never written my signature so many times as the year my daughter was in the sixth-grade integrative curriculum class. But I was also the best informed that year about what was happening in her school life."

Even though this curriculum change was completely teacher and student generated, our administrators were extremely supportive. They encouraged us to attend workshops, enroll in courses, and visit other schools. No actual professional development was provided for us by the district; so we created our own.

The seventh-grade teachers of our former students often told us that our students were on par with previous seventh graders in most areas, but performed well beyond expectations in others. Their research and computer skills were much more highly developed than in previous years, and students were anxious to get into more depth with their projects and assignments. Students also noted that in more traditional classrooms they did more homework than in their integrative curriculum year, but when pressed they admitted that homework meant "worksheets and stuff like that." They knew they took work home with us, but they saw it as "real work," relevant to their projects, unlike the "busy work" they associated with traditional homework.

I'm often asked about the benefits of this curriculum for students, but everyone tends to overlook the benefits for teachers. One of the biggest revelations for me has been the advantage of working as part of a "true" middle school team. Dennis and I had been a team (at least in name only) for many years and had always been quite successful, but we still retreated into our core subject areas for individual planning. When we began to look at the curriculum "givens" to see how they fit with the student-generated themes, we realized that the focus on curriculum was the glue that made us a team. When we combined our expertise, we found that we were much more creative and could help and support each other.

I also found that this curriculum process revives teachers. We tend to get into ruts of teaching the same thing year after year. Not so in this type of curriculum! When we begin a new school year, we really don't know what the curriculum themes would be. We had some predetermined skills and topics, but we needed the students to help generate the year's curriculum. It was as varied and as exciting for us as for our students as we watched a whole new year unfold in front of us and we knew it would be different from any of the previous years. Even though we knew that certain academic topics and skills would be included, it was interesting to see where they could best fit in from year to year. One year, statistics, graphs, and charts fell into the Crime Unit. Another year students placed the same areas of study in the Future Unit.

For an integrative curriculum to be truly successful, it takes total commitment. You can't just dabble with it. Students' concerns must be given serious consideration and validated as legitimate. Modeling is critical. We don't need to throw out successful teaching strategies we have used in the past. We still use large and small-group instruction, as well as lecture when appropriate. We must, however, let go of some things we may have considered sacred in our old curriculum. We have to weigh the value of everything we do. The time we have with our young adolescents is much too valuable to squander. We found that when all is said and done, our students learned even more in our student-oriented program than in previous years. Skills and content just seemed to fit in naturally. They took on added significance for students when they were used to answer students' own questions. Problem solving and social skills become an integrated part of every school day. For us, this experience was yet another lesson in how "less can be more."

As I have talked to educators over the years about our integrated program, many have suggested we would not have been so successful in the world of standards we have today. I disagree! We had givens, which were actually standards of what we expected students to know and be able to do at the end of each school year. We had our givens long before standards were the "in thing" to do. Students were very clear on what was expected of them and what they were to learn in their year with us. The only difference was that our students were part of the decision-making process—how they were going to learn—and they had to show us what they had learned. As this book illustrates, our students were involved in all aspects of their education for that year. We were a true learning community.

In reviewing the "Lessons Learned" section of this book, I firmly believe the lessons are still as true today as they were when the book was originally published. To validate this belief, I asked several teachers to look them over and give me feedback. Each teacher felt the lessons were true for the students in their classes, and several were amazed to find out the lessons had been set forth more than a decade ago. If the curriculum and middle level program is relevant, integrative, developmentally responsive, and sets high expectations and holds all members of the learning community to these standards, students will be successful on any assessments they are asked to undergo.

I have only to look at my colleagues Mark Springer, Theresa Kane, and Sherry Littlefield who are still in classrooms working with standards, local, state, and federal assessments, as these involve their students in integrative programs. Their students also do well on the assessments that are required of them, but also are becoming lifelong learners and very involved in their education. Just looking at the work students can do lets me know that I can return to the classroom, involve students in integrative curriculum, hold high expectations for our work together, and be sure they meet any standards as well. ◆

References

Alexander, W. (1993). Team organization: Taking steps beyond the interdisciplinary unit. *Journal of The New England League Of Middle Schools, VI*(3), 5-7.

Beane, J. A. (1993). *A middle school curriculum: From rhetoric to reality.* Columbus, OH: National Middle School Association.

Beane, J.A. (2005). *A reason to teach: Creating classrooms of dignity and hope*. Portsmouth, NH: Heinemann.

Bishop, P., & Allen-Malley, G. (2004). *The power of two: Partner teams in action*. Westerville, OH: National Middle School Association.

Brazee, E., & Capelluti, J. (1995). *Dissolving boundaries: Toward an integrative curriculum*. Columbus, OH: National Middle School Association.

Dewey, J. (1938). *Experience and education*. New York: Macmillan Publishing Company.

Springer, M. (1994). *Watershed: A successful voyage into integrative learning*. Columbus, OH: National Middle School Association.

Springer, M. (2006). *Soundings: A democratic, student-centered education*. Westerville, OH: National Middle School Association.

Stevenson C., & Carr, J. F. (1993). *Integrated studies in the middle grades: Dancing through walls*. New York: Teachers College Press.

Wiggington, E. (1985). *Sometimes a shining moment: The Foxfire experience*. Garden City, NY: Anchor/Doubleday.

Zessoules, R., & Gardner, H. (1991). Authentic assessment: Beyond the buzzword and into the classroom. In V. Perrone (Ed.), *Expanding student assessment* (pp. 47-71). Alexandria, VA: Association for Supervision and Curriculum Development.

Additional Resources on Integrated Curriculum

Watershed: A Successful Voyage into Integrative Learning,
by Mark Springer.

The dream of a fully integrative curriculum is achievable as chronicled by the author of this full-day, experiential program in which 40 motivated seventh graders use real-life activities and become responsible for their own education.

The Story of Alpha: A Multiage, Student-Centered Team—
33 Years and Counting, by Susan Kuntz.

This volume chronicles the history of a middle grades team in Vermont that uses a multiage and multiyear classroom, integrated curriculum, and student-driven goal setting to truly set it apart from other classrooms.

A Middle School Curriculum: From Rhetoric to Reality,
by James A. Beane.

This is the book that has initiated serious and continuing discussions about middle school curriculum and the limited effectiveness of subject-centered organization. A book of major importance, it presents a student-centered approach that has become the model for a fully integrative curriculum.

Curriculum Integration: Twenty Questions–With Answers,
by Gert Nesin and John Lounsbury.

Twenty of the most frequently asked questions about curriculum integration are answered in this resource for teachers and teams moving toward integrated curriculum. This small book provides a strong rationale and encourages teachers to discover the benefits when kids become active participants in their own learning.

Soundings: A Democratic, Student-Centered Education,
by Mark Springer.

Soundings provides a vicarious visit to a vibrant, highly successful school program that is "middle school" in its every aspect. Here is that fully detailed and illustrated example that is needed to inform and inspire—that rhetoric in practice to hold up for examination and emulation.

A Reason to Teach: Creating Classrooms of Dignity and Hope, by James A. Beane.

A Reason to Teach is written for teachers who want to bring democratic teaching to their classrooms and schools. All ideas are illustrated with vibrant examples from real classrooms around the country, including an extended case study of how one teacher and his students in a large city organized their curriculum around the goal of getting a new school for their neighborhood. Practical and principled, this book shows the how, the why, and the power of the democratic way.

This We Believe in Action, Thomas O. Erb, Editor.

This resource explains to educators, parents, and policymakers what truly successful middle level schools can be. The 14 characteristics identified in National Middle School Association's position paper, *This We Believe: Successful Schools for Young Adolescents*, are described in individual chapters and illustrated with photographs from the accompanying DVD. The DVD itself provides compelling scenes from eight highly successful middle level schools across the country, showing how the schools are implementing these 14 characteristics.

(To order these and other NMSA publications, call 1-800-528-6672 or visit our Web site at www.nmsa.org)